SCIENCE AROUND US

Amphibians

By Peter Murray

THE CHILD'S WORLD®
CHANHASSEN, MINNESOTA

The Child's World

Published in the United States of America by The Child's World®
PO Box 326, Chanhassen, MN 55317-0326
800-599-READ
www.childsworld.com

Content Advisers:
Jim Rising, PhD,
Professor of Zoology,
University of Toronto,
Department of Zoology,
Toronto, Ontario,
Canada, and Trudy
Rising, Educational
Consultant, Toronto,
Ontario, Canada

Photo Credits:
Cover/frontispiece: Darren Maybury; Eye Ubiquitous/Corbis; cover corner: Corbis.
Interior: Animals Animals/Earth Scenes: 12 (Juan Manuel Renjifo), 17 (David M.
Dennis), 25 (Peter Weimann), 27 (Marian Bacon), 29 (Doug Wechsler); Corbis: 7
(Jonathan Blair), 11 (Rod Patterson; Gallo Images), 16 (Joe McDonald), 19 (Kevin R.
Morris), 21 (Buddy Mays); Thomas R. Jones/Dembinsky Photo Associates: 14; Dwight
R. Kuhn: 18, 24; Carmela Leszczynski/Animals Animals/Earth Scenes: 6, 20; Todd
Marshall: 4; Gary Meszaros/Dembinsky Photo Associates: 9, 15, 23; John
Mielcarek/Dembinsky Photo Associates: 8, 26.

The Child's World®: Mary Berendes, Publishing Director

Editorial Directions, Inc.: E. Russell Primm, Editorial Director; Pam Rosenberg, Line
Editor; Katie Marsico, Assistant Editor; Matt Messbarger, Editorial Assistant; Susan
Hindman, Copy Editor; Susan Ashley, Proofreader; Peter Garnham, Terry Johnson,
Olivia Nellums, Katherine Trickle, and Stephen Carl Wender, Fact Checkers; Tim
Griffin/IndexServ, Indexer; Cian Loughlin O'Day, Photo Researcher; Linda S. Koutris,
Photo Selector

The Design Lab: Kathleen Petelinsek, Design and Page Production

Library of Congress Cataloging-in-Publication Data
Murray, Peter, 1952 Sept. 29–
  Amphibians / by Peter Murray.
    p. cm. — (Science around us)
  Includes bibliographical references and index.
  ISBN 1-59296-271-8 (lib. bd. : alk. paper) 1. Amphibians—Juvenile literature.
[1. Amphibians.] I. Title. II. Science around us (Child's World (Firm)
  QL644.2.M86 2004
  597.8—dc22   2003027222

TABLE OF CONTENTS

CHAPTER ONE

THE FOUR-FOOTED FISH

bout 365 million years ago, before dinosaurs ruled Earth, an air-breathing fish dragged itself out of the water. It waded onto shore with its four powerful, fleshy fins. Scientists believe that this nameless walking fish was the ancestor of all the scaly, feathered,

Scientists believe that amphibians evolved from ancient fish.

and furry creatures that came later. They think that all frogs, turtles, dinosaurs, chickens, dogs, and even human beings **evolved** from this common ancestor.

Why would any fish leave the water?

The move from water to dry land probably got its start during ancient **droughts.** As the ponds and streams **evaporated,** most of the fish in those drying pools died. But some gulped air when they couldn't get enough oxygen from the muddy water. They were able to absorb enough oxygen from the air to survive.

Lungfish are able to breathe both air and water. When their pond dries out, they bury themselves in a cocoon of mud and mucus to wait for rain. Lungfish live in Africa, South America, and Australia.

Inside the bodies of those early air-gulpers, oxygen-absorbing pockets—an early kind of lungs—began to form. Some of these fish developed powerful fins. They used their

Mudskippers are fish that live in swampy areas. They can climb and walk about when they are out of the water.

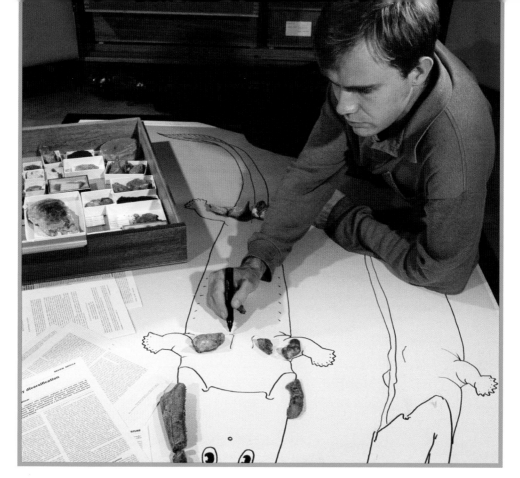

Scientists use fossils to help them find out what the earliest amphibians looked like.

fins like legs to move from one pond to another, gulping air as they

made their way across dry land.

Slowly, over tens of millions of years, these four-limbed, air-

breathing fish adapted to living on both land and in the water. Their

fins evolved into jointed legs. They found new sources of food on

land. They became the first amphibians.

CHAPTER TWO

LIVING TWO LIVES

Fish, reptiles, and amphibians are all cold-blooded **verte-brates** with highly developed nervous systems, two eyes, jaws, and teeth. So what makes amphibians different?

The word amphibian means "living two lives." Most amphibians live part of their lives in the water and part on land. One of the best examples of this is the common leopard frog.

Leopard frogs can be found in lakes and ponds throughout North America. They begin life much like

Leopard frogs are predators whose diet consists mainly of insects such as beetles, flies, and ants.

Leopard frog tadpoles hatch in spring and change into adult frogs in the summer. Larger animals often eat tadpoles and young frogs.

One frog can lay thousands of eggs. Many of them will be eaten by birds, fish, and other amphibians before they hatch. Young tadpoles also are often eaten by fish, birds, and other hungry predators. Only a few will survive to become adult frogs.

their fish ancestors, from a mass of soft eggs laid in the water. If you look around the edges of ponds in the spring, you can often find jellylike masses of leopard frog eggs.

The frog eggs soon hatch into larvae. Frog larvae are also known as tadpoles. Tadpoles look like tiny fish, with finned tails, gills, and no legs. Young tadpoles feed on algae scraped from leaves, sticks, and rocks.

Over the next two to three months, the tadpole grows. Its gills are replaced by air-breathing lungs. Tiny legs appear on each side of its tail, and the tail is slowly absorbed into its body. About three months after hatching, the tadpole has slowly become a frog. This is called **metamorphosis.** Salamanders undergo a similar metamorphosis from tadpole to adult.

About 4,500 **species** of amphibians live on Earth today, including frogs, toads, salamanders, newts, and the wormlike caecilians.

All amphibians have a few things in common. They are vertebrates. They are ectothermic, or cold-blooded—their body temperature rises and falls with the air temperature. Adult amphibians are carnivores—they eat other animals, including insects, worms, crustaceans, fish, and other amphibians. Unlike reptiles and most fish, amphibians do not have scales.

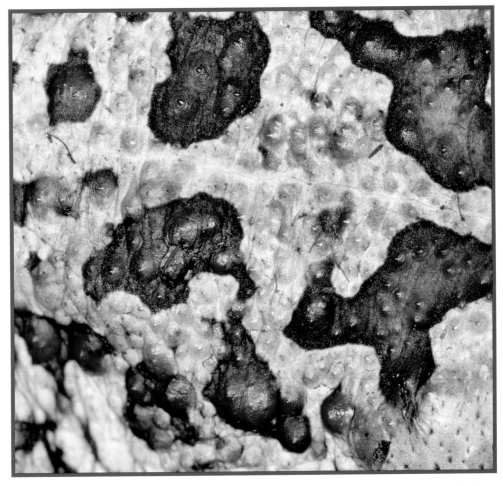

This close-up view of toad skin shows that toads, like other amphibians, do not have scaly skin.

In other ways, amphibians are as different from one another as people are from chickens. What does a 3-kilogram (7-pound) goliath frog have in common with a 13-centimeter-long (5-inch-long) legless, blind, subterranean caecilian? Not a whole lot!

CHAPTER THREE

THE CAECILIANS

Caecilians are legless, burrowing amphibians that live in the warm parts of South America, Africa, and Southeast Asia. They spend most of their time underground. If you saw one, you would probably mistake it for a big worm.

Caecilians live in warm tropical areas and look a lot like worms.

Scientists have identified 165 species of caecilians. Because caecilians are so secretive, there are probably more species yet to be found. The largest caecilians can grow up to $1^1/_2$ meters (5 feet) in length, while the smallest species are less than 13 centimeters (5 inches) long.

Caecilians are completely legless. Above ground, they move across the surface like wriggling eels. When burrowing, they push their way through loose soil by ramming their heads forward, then pulling their bodies along, much like earthworms.

So what makes a caecilian different from a worm? If you pick one up, you'll find out soon enough! Caecilians have powerful jaws and a large mouth lined with sharp teeth. They feed on insects, worms, frogs, and lizards.

Unlike frogs and salamanders, most caecilians give birth to live

Caecilians have large mouths and sharp teeth. They use their heads to burrow through the soil.

young. Their eggs hatch inside their bodies, and the baby caecilians look like small adults—there is no larval stage.

Because caecilians live underground in the tropics, they are difficult to study. Much remains to be learned about how they live.

CHAPTER FOUR

SALAMANDERS AND NEWTS

Salamanders and newts look like slimy, smooth-skinned, slow-moving, long-tailed lizards. They live in moist areas throughout much of the world. There are more than 400 different species of salamanders and newts, from the tiny 1-centimeter-long ($^1/_2$-inch-long) lungless salamanders

This red eft is a young red-spotted newt. These amphibians start their lives as tadpole-like creatures in the water. After they develop legs, they live on land for 2 to 7 years. Then they return to the water where they live the rest of their lives as adult red-spotted newts.

of southern Mexico to the 70-kilogram (154-pound) Chinese great

salamander.

Like frogs, salamanders and newts begin life as masses of soft,

jellylike eggs. The eggs hatch into water-

breathing, fishlike larvae that look much

like tadpoles. The larvae slowly change

What is the difference between salamanders and newts? Newt is the name for certain species of salamander that spend most of their lives in the water. Most newts are small and brightly colored.

A Jefferson salamander (above) lays between 150 and 300 eggs in the spring. The eggs will hatch into larvae and the larvae will become adult salamanders in 2 to 4 months.

The hellbender is a salamander that lives its entire life in the water.

into adults. Their gills and fins disappear, and they grow legs.

Most salamanders live their adult lives on land. Some salamanders have lungs. Others absorb oxygen only through their skin and the linings of their mouths.

Salamanders eat insects, worms, and other small animals. Large salamanders such as the hellbender will eat larger animals, including fish, frogs, birds, and other salamanders.

Salamanders live in moist areas and can often be found hiding under leaves.

Salamanders keep their skin moist at all times. They are most

active when the sun is down. During the day, you can find salaman-

ders hiding under rocks, logs, and wet leaves.

CHAPTER FIVE

FROGS AND TOADS

Thestatic jumping, croaking, goggle-eyed, tail-less amphibians live in just about every part of the world. Only the frozen polar regions and the driest deserts have no frogs or toads.

A frog rests on a lily pad in a pond in Thailand.

There are nearly 4,000 species of frogs and toads. All of them—from the 1-centimeter-long ($^1/_2$-inch-long) brachycephalid frog of Brazil to Africa's 75-centimeter-long (30-inch-long) goliath frog—have the same general shape. Even the strangest-looking frogs still look like frogs!

Some people call the ornate horned frog the "Pac-man frog" because of its large mouth.

The poison on the skin of poison arrow frogs is so strong that just holding one of them in your hand can be dangerous.

What's the difference between frogs and toads? Herpetologists—scientists who study amphibians and reptiles—consider toads to be a type of frog. Toad is simply the common name for frogs with dry, bumpy skin and short legs.

In many ways, however, frogs are quite different from one another. The common American toad has bumpy, mottled skin that keeps it hidden from larger predators. The poison arrow frogs of the tropics take the opposite approach. Their bright colors let predators know that they are poisonous—their skin contains a deadly **toxin.**

Frogs are our most familiar amphibians. They are active during the day, and are often seen swimming and hopping near the shore of ponds and streams. We also know frogs are present because they are NOISY!

In spring and early summer, the wetlands are filled with the peeping, croaking, and chirping of frogs. Frogs are noisiest during the mating season. Male frogs make a tremendous racket to attract female frogs. Their voices also warn other males to stay away from their territory. Every frog species has its own special voice.

The tiny, brown spring peeper makes a high-pitched chirping sound. During the mating season, thousands of peepers will call out at once, making a deafening noise. The bullfrog, a much larger frog, speaks with a deeper voice that sounds like *jug-a-rum, jug-a-rum.*

Like all amphibians, adult frogs are carnivores. Insects and worms are their favorite foods, but frogs have been known to devour almost anything that will fit in their mouths, including crayfish, birds, tadpoles, fish, snails, and small rodents.

Insects, such as the dragonfly being eaten by this green frog, are a favorite food of frogs.

CHAPTER SIX

A Future for Amphibians?

Amphibians are the most ancient four-legged, land-dwelling

creatures on Earth. They have survived longer than any other

land-dwelling vertebrate, but they are also the most sensitive to

changes in their environment.

Spotted salamanders live on land, usually in forests, but return to ponds in wetlands to deposit their eggs. People need to protect forest and wetland habitats to help make sure that these salamanders can survive.

When rain forests are cut down, the birds that lived there may be able to fly to another forest. Mammals can travel hundreds of miles to find new homes. But salamanders, frogs, and caecilians cannot escape the

When people cut down too many trees in the rainforests, many amphibian species cannot survive.

destruction. Many rain forest species are in danger of **extinction.**

When rivers and lakes are polluted, many creatures suffer. Amphibians feel it more than others. Their moist skin absorbs toxins directly from the air and water. Amphibians are sometimes called

A dead green frog floats in polluted water. Amphibians are often the first living things to get sick from pollution in the air or water.

Prionosuchus, the largest known amphibian, was up to 10 meters (33 feet) long. It looked like a giant salamander with alligator jaws. But you don't need to worry about running into this amphibian—Prionosuchus has been extinct for hundreds of millions of years.

indicator species because when something goes wrong with the water or air, amphibians are often the first to get sick.

Many years ago, coal miners used to take a caged canary into the mines with them. When the air in the mine shaft started to go bad, the canary would fall over dead. The miners would know that if they didn't get out of the mine soon, they would be next to die.

Amphibians are the canaries of the natural world. When frogs and salamanders start disappearing, it is a message to us all.

Tree frogs, such as this gliding frog from Indonesia, spend much of their time in trees and use their webbed hands and feet to help them glide from tree to tree.

GLOSSARY

droughts (DROUTS) Long periods of very dry weather are called droughts.

evaporated (i-VAP-uh-rate-ed) If a liquid has evaporated, it has turned into a vapor or gas.

evolved (ih-VOLVD) Something that has evolved has changed slowly over time.

extinction (ex-STINK-shun) Extinction is the process of a species dying out.

metamorphosis (met-uh-MOR-fuh-sis) Metamorphosis is the series of changes that some animals go through as they develop from eggs to larvae to adults.

species (SPEE-sheez) A species is a certain type of living thing. Only amphibians of the same species can mate and produce young together.

toxin (TOK-sin) A toxin is a substance that is poisonous.

vertebrates (VUR-tuh-brayts) Vertebrates are animals with backbones and internal skeletons. Mammals, birds, reptiles, amphibians, and fish are all vertebrates.

▶ There are several differences between amphibians and fish. Amphibians can breathe air; most fish breathe water. Amphibians have legs; fish have fins. Amphibians have eyelids; fish don't have eyelids. Amphibians have smooth skin; fish have scales.

▶ Some salamanders never metamorphose—they just get bigger! The adult axolotl looks much like its larva, with a large head, external gills, and a finned tail. Axolotls spend their entire lives in the water.

▶ Hellbenders and their relatives are large aquatic salamanders with loose, wrinkled skin. Hellbenders, which can grow to nearly 1 meter (3 feet) long, live in mountain streams in the eastern United States. The giant salamanders of China get even bigger—up to 2 meters (6 feet) in length.

▶ Poison arrow frogs come in a variety of bright colors and markings.

▶ The cane toad has a monster appetite—rats, birds, and even turtles are on the cane toad's menu. Cane toads don't have to avoid being eaten themselves. They secrete a powerful poison from glands on their shoulders. Any animal that tries to eat a cane toad will get sick and may even die.

Cane toads were brought into Australia in the 1930s by the sugar cane industry. It was hoped that their large appetites would help control two kinds of beetles that feed on sugar cane. The toads were not successful in controlling the beetle pests, but there are now so many cane toads in Australia that they are considered pests!

VERTEBRATES

fish

amphibians

reptiles

birds

mammals

INVERTEBRATES

sponges

worms

insects

spiders & scorpions

mollusks & crustaceans

sea stars

sea jellies

HOW TO LEARN MORE ABOUT AMPHIBIANS

At the Library

Cassie, Brian. *National Audubon Society First Field Guide: Amphibians.*
New York: Scholastic, 1999.

Miller, Sara Swan. *Amazing Amphibians.*
New York: Franklin Watts, 2001.

Woods, Samuel G., and Jeff Cline (illustrator). *The Amazing Book of
Reptile and Amphibian Records: The Largest, the Fastest, the Most
Poisonous, and Many More!* Woodbridge, Conn.: Blackbirch, 2000.

On the Web

VISIT OUR HOME PAGE FOR LOTS OF LINKS ABOUT AMPHIBIANS:
http://www.childsworld.com/links.html
Note to Parents, Teachers, and Librarians: We routinely check our Web links to make
sure they're safe, active sites—so encourage your readers to check them out!

Places to Visit or Contact

AMERICAN MUSEUM OF NATURAL HISTORY
To learn more about reptiles and amphibians
Central Park West at 79th Street
New York, NY 10024
212/769-5000

THE FIELD MUSEUM
To see the museum's exhibit on Reptiles and Amphibians
1400 South Lake Shore Drive
Chicago, IL 60605
312/922-9410

INDEX

About the Author

Peter Murray has written more than 80 children's books on science, nature, history, and other topics. An animal lover, Pete lives in Golden Valley, Minnesota, in a house with one woman, two poodles, several dozen spiders, thousands of microscopic dust mites, and an occasional mouse.